An Animal Family

BEARS AND CUBS

By Polly LeChance

Gareth Stevens Publishing

Please visit our website, www.garethstevens.com. For a free color catalog of all our high-quality books, call toll free 1-800-542-2595 or fax 1-877-542-2596.

Cataloging-in-Publication Data

Names: LeChance, Polly.
Title: Bears and cubs / Polly LeChance.
Description: New York : Gareth Stevens Publishing, 2018. | Series: An animal family | Includes index.
Identifiers: ISBN 9781482463699 (pbk.) | ISBN 9781482463712 (library bound) | ISBN 9781482463705 (6 pack)
Subjects: LCSH: Bears–Juvenile literature. | Bear cubs–Juvenile literature. | Parental behavior in animals–Juvenile literature.
Classification: LCC QL737.C27 L43 2018 | DDC 599.78–dc23

First Edition

Published in 2018 by
Gareth Stevens Publishing
111 East 14th Street, Suite 349
New York, NY 10003

Editor: Ryan Nagelhout
Designer: Samantha DeMartin

Photo credits: Cover, p. 1 Debbie Steinhausser/Shutterstock.com; p. 5 Ondrej Prosicky/Shutterstock.com; p. 7 (left) Gerald Marella/Shutterstock.com; p. 7 (bottom right) Zhiltsov Alexandr/Shutterstock.com; p. 7 (top right) Laura Mountainspring/Shutterstock.com; p. 9 Menno Schaefer/Shutterstock.com; p. 11 Tom Reichner/Shutterstock.com; pp. 13, 14 (grizzly bears) Tony Campbell/Shutterstock.com; p. 15 Vladimir Wrangel/Shutterstock.com; p. 17 Dennis W Donohue/Shutterstock.com; pp. 19, 24 (cubs) Giedriius/Shutterstock.com; pp. 21, 24 (polar bears) Christopher Wood/Shutterstock.com; p. 23 Greg and Jan Ritchie/Shutterstock.com.

Printed in the United States of America

CPSIA compliance information: Batch #CS17GS: For further information contact Gareth Stevens, New York, New York at 1-800-542-2595.

Contents

Bears are big animals.

They are many different colors.

Some bears are white.
These are polar bears.

Black bears love to climb trees.

Brown bears love to swim.

They are also called grizzly bears.

Baby bears
are called cubs!

They love to play.

Cubs follow
their mothers.

They learn to find
food to eat.
This is called hunting.

Words to Know

cubs

grizzly bears

polar bears

Index